The Character & Faith Of Robert E. Lee

In His Own Words

Edited by Curt Steger

May you find the words and
Character of Robert E. Lee true.

Curt Steger
Manassas Battlefield
Manassas, Va.

The Character & Faith of Robert E. Lee
In His Own Words

Copyright ©2002 Curt Steger. 4rd Printing. All rights
reserved.

Designed by K. D. Estell: Loyal Arts & Letters
www.loyalpublishing.com

Cover Photo of Robert B. Lee courtesy of
Alabama Department of Archives and History,
Montgomery, Alabama

Cover Photo of Robert E. Lee Statue courtesy of
San Diego Historical Society Photograph Collection.

This book about "character" and "faith" is dedicated to my children Chris, Mark, Mary Ann, and Ryan and to their loving mother, Ann. May our family always seek both.

It is also dedicated to the memory of my mother, Adelle Gatewood Steger.

FOR SPEAKING ENGAGEMENTS
&
OTHER LEE ITEMS BELOW

By Curt Steger

VISIT
Curt Steger's Robert E. Lee Store
www.releestore.com

Guiding Principles of Robert E. Lee
Spiritual Guide of Robert. E. Lee
Who Is This Man Robert E. Lee?
The Robert E. Lee Gentleman
A General's Prayer
Lee's Last Prayer
A Prayer For Life
Annie's Prayer

1-888-498-9364
431 Vista Court, Mt. Sterling, Kentucky 40353

CONTENTS

95 Who Is This Man Robert E. Lee?

125 Endnotes

ACKNOWLEDGMENTS

I am delighted to express my appreciation to so many wonderflul people that I have met during the last two-and-a-half years while doing research for this book I am deeply grateful to Patricia Hobbs, Director of Lee Chapel and Vaughan Stanley, Special Collections/Reference Librarian, Leyburn Library at Washington and Lee University.

I am particularly grateful to Lisa McCown, appropriately given the nickname "The Angel of Lexington", and the Special Collections Assistant at the Leyburn Library at Washington and Lee.

I extend to Mart Jacobson and Loyal Publishing of Sisters, Oregon a very special thank you.

I also wish to express my appreciation to both the Leyburn Library at Washington and Lee University and the Mt. Sterling-Montgomery County Library in Mt. Sterling, Kentucky.

My wife, Ann, and I are grateful to Peg Braford for her generosity in allowing us to stay the numerous times in her beautiful bed and breakfast cottage at Natural Bridge, Virginia, which we have grown to love and cherish.

Lastly, I am forever grateful for the love and support of Ann and her belief that a book about character is important—not only for our children and grandchildren, but for everyone's children and grandchildren.

CHARACTER

★ ★ ★

"When the future historian comes to survey the character of Lee he will find it rising like a huge mountain above the undulating plain of humanity, and he will have to lift his eyes toward heaven to catch its summit. He possessed every virtue of the great commanders, without treachery; a private citizen without wrong; a neighbor without reproach; a Christian without hypocrisy, and a man without guile."

— Honorable B. H. Hill

Speech delivered in Atlana Georgia
shortly after Lee's death [182]

". . . I have to labour for my living and I am ashamed to do nothing that will give me honest support." [1]

"You must endeavour to enjoy the pleasure of doing good. That is all that makes life valuable." [2]

". . . study human nature, more by experience than by precept . . . learn . . . not to be deceived by the low, the cunning, & the envious." [3]

Securing Happiness

"My Beautiful Daughter: ... I hope everything is agreeable, and that you are becoming more and more interested in making those around you happy. That is the true way to secure your own happiness..." [4]

"A farmer's motto should be 'Toil and Trust.'" [5]

"You must make friends while you are young, that you may enjoy them when old." [6]

"We must all do what promises the most usefulness." [7]

"Youth is so fleeting and life so short." [8]

JUDGING CHARACTER

"IT HAS BEEN SAID THAT OUR LETTERS ARE GOOD REPRESENTATIVES OF OUR MINDS. THEY CERTAINLY PRESENT A GOOD CRITERION FOR JUDGING OF THE CHARACTER OF THE INDIVIDUAL." [9]

"When a thing is done we ought always make the best of it." [10]

"The interests of all are inseparably connected…" [11]

"…I think every boy can be persuaded & led to do what is right by an affectionate & judicious mother." [12]

"…human virtue should equal human calamity." [13]

"Cleanliness, temperance & order [are] very promotive of health & cheerfulness." [14]

"My only object is to endeavor to make them [students at Washington College] see their true interest, to teach them to labor diligently for their improvement, and to prepare themselves for the great work of life." [15]

"I am one of those silly persons when I have any thing to do I can't rest satisfied till it has been accomplished." [16]

Endeavor to Improve

"My precious Annie: ...I hope you will always appear to me as you are now painted on my heart, and that you will endeavour to improve and so conduct yourself as to make you happy and me joyful all our lives. Diligent and earnest attention to all your duties can only accomplish this."[17]

"…the great duty of life is…the promotion of the happiness and welfare of our fellow men." [18]

"Duty…is the sublimest word in our language. Do your duty in all things…. You cannot do more, you should never do less." [19]

"You must be aware of one thing, that those you deal with will consider their advantage and not yours. So, while being fair and just, you must not neglect your interests" [20]

"You will have to get married if you wish to prosper…" [21]

"…the greater difficulties in our lives the harder must we strive for success." [22]

"…in your youth you must be careful to discipline your thoughts, words, and actions." [23]

Habituate Yourself

"Habituate yourself to useful employment, regular improvement, and to the benefit of all those around you..." [24]

"Hold on to your purity and virtue. They will proudly sustain you in all trials and difficulties, and cheer you in every calamity." [25]

"We must not for own pleasure lose sight of the interest of our children." [26]

"Do not worry yourself about things you can not help…" [27]

"…it is the part of benevolence to aid all we can and sympathize with all who are in need, it is the part of wisdom to attend to our own affairs." [28]

"Lay nothing too much to heart." [29]

"Desire nothing too eagerly, nor think that all things can be perfectly accomplished according to our own notions." [30]

"Drive all your work with judgment and energy." [31]

"Education embraces the physical, moral and intellectual instruction of a child from infancy to manhood. Any system is imperfect which does not combine them all." [32]

Parenting

"Neither violence nor harshness should ever be used [in child rearing], and the parent must bear constantly in mind, that to govern his child, he must show him that he can control himself." [33]

"Time…brings a cure to all things…." [34]

"Do not go out to many parties, preserve your simple tastes and manners, and you will enjoy more pleasure." [35]

"Plainess and simplicity of dress, early hours, and rational amusements, I wish you to practice." [36]

"It is the Substance, not the Show I desire for him. If he cannot, or will not, attain the former, I wish him to abandon the chase of the latter." [37]

"[The exercise of self-denial and self-control] is the true means of establishing a virtuous character, so far as it can be accomplished by human means." [38]

"I commend you for not wishing to go in debt, or to proceed faster in your operations than prudence dictates." [39]

"We must make up our minds to meet with reverses and overcome them." [40]

"It is necessary we should be humble and taught to be less boastful, less selfish, and more devoted to right and justice to all the world." [41]

"…oppose constancy to adversity, fortitude to suffering, and courage to danger…" [42]

"You must be diligent in the instruction of your children, & begin by teaching them the great love of God for them, his kindness to all his people, where he never affects but for their good…" [43]

"I am cheered in my downward path in life by the onward and rising course of my dear sons." [44]

"…do your best, and I shall be satisfied." [45]

"It is persuasion and not force….Cultivate the powers of pleasing." [46]

"It is to men…of high integrity and commanding intellect that the country must look to give character to her councils." [47]

"In my own case I would rather be in a hut with my own family than in a palace with others." [48]

"I cannot consent to receive pay for services I do not render!" [49]

"We must aid our friends all we can." [50]

"...no honest man can take long to deliberate which side he will choose." [51]

Prosperity and Advancement

"My dear Fitzhugh:...You know the interest I take in your prosperity and advancement, which cannot be assured without earnest attention to your business on your part, and therefore I never urge you to act contrary to your own judgment in reference to them."[52]

Unbecoming

"I KNOW HOW PRONE WE ARE TO CENSURE
AND HOW READY TO BLAME OTHERS
FOR THE NON-FULFILMENT OF OUR
EXPECTATIONS. THIS IS UNBECOMING IN
A GENEROUS PEOPLE, AND I GRIEVE TO SEE
ITS EXPRESSION." [53]

" I feel sensibly, in my old age, the absence of my children." [54]

"To succeed it is necessary to set the example [of having discipline]...." [55]

"What...most lack is the pains & labour of incubating discipline. It is a painful tedious process...." [56]

"It is particularly incumbent on those charged with the instruction of the youth to set them an example of submission to authority...." [57]

"…there is no labour so beneficient, so elevated and so sublime, as the teaching of salvation to every man." [58]

"I think it better to do right, even if we suffer in so doing, than to incur the reproach of our consciences…" [59]

"…it is satisfactory always to have facts to go on; they restrain supposition and conjecture, confirm faith, and bring contentment." [60]

GLOOMY FEELINGS

"SHAKE OFF THOSE GLOOMY FEELINGS. DRIVE THEM AWAY. FIX YOUR MIND & PLEASURES UPON WHAT IS BEFORE YOU.... ALL IS BRIGHT IF YOU WILL THINK IT SO. ALL IS HAPPY IF YOU WILL MAKE IT SO. DO NOT DREAM. IT IS TOO IDEAL. TOO IMAGINARY, DREAMING BY DAY, I MEAN. LIVE IN THE WORLD YOU INHABIT. LOOK UPON THINGS AS THEY ARE. TAKE THEM AS YOU FIND THEM. MAKE THE BEST OF THEM, TURN THEM TO YOUR ADVANTAGE. [61]

"Sad thoughts…are necessary & good for us. They cause us to reflect….Do not yield to them. But use them as a medium through which to view life correctly." [62]

"No one will attend to your business as well as you will yourself…." [63]

"War is a terrible alternative & should be the very, very last resort." [64]

"We must be very careful how we are influenced by hearsay." [65]

"I do not care for display." [66]

"Charity should have no beginning or ending." [67]

"…I must not consent to do aught that would lower me in your eyes, my own & that of others…." [68]

"Practice self-denial and self-control, as well as the strictest economy in all financial matters." [69]

"Above all, [the teacher] must be uniform, consistent, firm & kind in his conduct & teach more by acts than by ends." [70]

"We have no printed rules. We have but one rule here, [Washington College] and it is that every student must be a gentleman." [71]

"I cannot see what you are proud of & advise you against all such feelings for you know what is said in that good book about a proud spirit going before a fall." [72]

"We must expect reverses, even defeats. They are sent to teach us wisdom and prudence, to call forth greater energies, and to prevent our falling into greater disasters." [73]

"I consider the character of no man affected by a want of success provided he has made an honest effort to succeed." [74]

Do What You Ought

"THE STRUGGLE WHICH YOU DESCRIBE YOUR EXPERIENCE BETWEEN DOING WHAT YOU OUGHT AND WHAT YOU DESIRE IS COMMON TO ALL. YOU HAVE ONLY ALWAYS TO DO WHAT IS RIGHT. IT WILL BECOME EASIER BY PRACTICE, AND YOU WILL ALWAYS ENJOY IN THE MIDST OF YOUR TRIALS THE PLEASURE OF AN APPROVING CONSCIENCE. THAT WILL BE WORTH EVERYTHING ELSE." [75]

"…the more you know, the more you find there is to know in this grand & beautiful world." [76]

"You will find all the day of your life that there is much to learn & much to do…. You will find in afterlife you cannot know too much." [77]

"…when a man desires to do a thing, or when a thing gives a man pleasure, he requires but small provocation to induce him to do it." [78]

"…take a happier view of things & do not be dissatisfied because they do not accord more nearly with your views & wishes." [79]

"We rarely know what is good for us & rarely see things as they really exist, so clouded is our vision by narrow selfishness, & often complain of what we ought not & blame others when the fault is on ourselves." [80]

"…meet with a smiling face & cheerful heart the vicissitudes of life…." [81]

"…what I want to learn is to apply what I already know." [82]

"The law should not be open to the charge of partiality…." [83]

"The education of a man or woman is never completed till they die. There is always before them much to learn and more to do. Our hardest lesson is self-knowledge, and it is one perhaps that is never accomplished." [84]

"My experience through life has convinced me that, while moderation and temperance in all things are commendable and beneficial, abstinence from spirituous liquors is the best safeguard of morals and health," [85]

"Men need no stimulant; it is something, I am persuaded, that they can do without" [86]

"Your riches consist in your children." [87]

"…we cannot undo the past; that is forever gone; but the future is in our hands…" [88]

"There is a true glory and a true honor; the glory of duty done—the honor of the integrity of principle." [89]

"I have a way of estimating young men which does not often fail me. I cannot note the conduct of any one, for even a brief period, without finding out what sort of a mother he had." [90]

"...always respect the religious views and feelings of other." [91]

"If you will act in accordance with the dictates of your conscience, to the best of your judgment...you will do right." [92]

"You must expect discomforts and annoyances all through life. No place or position is secure from them, and you must make up your mind to meet with them and bear them." [93]

"...if you are virtuous and laborious you will accomplish all the good you propose to yourself." [94]

"As a general principle, you should not force young men to do their duty, but let them do it voluntarily and thereby develop their characters….Make no needless rules." [95]

"Obedience to lawful authority is the foundation to manly character." [96]

"I think it better to avoid it (spirituous liquor) altogether, as its temperate use is so difficult." [97]

"Do not cherish bitterness." [98]

Your Mind

You will find it difficult, at first, to control the operation of your mind under all circumstances... but the power can be gained by determination and practice.... If it had not been for this power, I do not see how I could have stood what I had to go through with." [99]

TRUTH AND MANLINESS

"...TRUTH AND MANLINESS ARE TWO QUALITIES THAT WILL CARRY YOU THROUGH THIS WORLD MUCH BETTER THAN POLICY, ON TACT OR EXPEDIENCY, OR ANY OTHER WORD THAT WAS EVER DEVISED TO CONCEAL OR MYSTIFY A DEVIATION FROM A STRAIGHT LINE." [100]

"The main thing to be acquired consists in habits of industry and self-denial....The first business of education is to draw forth and put into habitual exercise the former dispositions, such as kindness, justice, and self-denial." [101]

"I delight to pay compliments to those so well deserving them...." [102]

"When a man makes a mistake, I call him to my tent, talk to him, and use the authority of my position to make him do the right thing the next time." [103]

Exceeding Your Means

" I hope you will continue never to exceed your means. It will save you much anxiety and mortification, and enable you to maintain your independence of character and feeling. It is easier to make our wishes conform to our means, than to make our means conform to our wishes. In fact, we want but little. Our happiness depends upon our independence, the success of our operations, prosperity of our plans, health, contentment, and the esteem of our friends, all of which, my dear son, I hope you will enjoy to the full..." [104]

WHAT'S IN A NAME

"IN A LETTER TO CHARLOTTE [HIS DAUGHTER-IN-LAW] WRITTEN SINCE MY RETURN, I EXPRESSED THE GRATIFICATION I FELT AT THE COMPLIMENT PAID ME IN YOUR INTENTION TO CALL MY FIRST GRANDCHILD AFTER ME. I WISH I COULD OFFER HIM A MORE WORTHY NAME AND A BETTER EXAMPLE. HE MUST ELEVATE THE FIRST AND MAKE USE OF THE LATTER TO VOID THE ERRORS I HAVE COMMITTED." [105]

"At times the temptation to relax will be hard upon you, but will grow feebler and more feeble by constant resistance...I know it will confirm you in your present resolve to try and do your best." [106]

"Hold yourself above every mean action. Be strictly honorable in every act, and be not ashamed to do right." [107]

"...you will endeavor to improve and so conduct yourself as to make you happy and me joyful all our lives." [108]

Written to his daughter, Annie, in 1853
When he was superintendent of West Point

Charity

"I AM MUCH OBLIGED TO YOU FOR YOUR KIND OFFER TO SEND ME A HAT, AND I APPRECIATE MOST HIGHLY THE MOTIVES WHICH PROMPTED IT. WHEN SO MANY ARE DESTITUTE, I DISLIKE TO HAVE MORE THAN I ACTUALLY REQUIRE, AND YET AM UNWILLING TO APPEAR INSENSIBLE TO YOUR SENTIMENTS OF FRIENDSHIP AND SYMPATHY, I HAVE A VERY GOOD HAT, WHICH WILL ANSWER MY PURPOSE THE WHOLE YEAR, AND I WOULD, THEREFORE, PREFER THAT YOU WOULD GIVE TO OTHERS WHAT I REALLY DO NOT REQUIRE." [109]

The Future

"No one can say what is in the future, nor is it wise to anticipate evil. But it is well to prepare for what may reasonably happen & be provided for the worst." [110]

"I feel that I have an incurable disease coming on me—old age. I would like to go to some quiet place in the country and rest." [111]

"My daily walks are alone, up and down the banks of the river, and my pleasure is derived from my own thoughts and from the sight of the flowers and animals I there meet with." [112]

"...nothing is more instructive than the perusal of the deeds of men in other ages." [113]

LOVE

"EXPERIENCE WILL TEACH YOU THAT, NOTWITHSTANDING ALL APPEARANCES TO THE CONTRARY, YOU WILL NEVER RECEIVE SUCH A LOVE AS IS FELT FOR YOU BY YOUR FATHER AND MOTHER. THAT LIVES THROUGH ABSENCE, DIFFICULTIES, AND TIME. YOUR OWN FEELINGS WILL TEACH YOU HOW IT SHOULD BE RETURNED AND APPRECIATED." [114]

A True Gentleman

"The forbearing use of power does not only form the touchstone, but the manner in which an individual enjoys certain advantages over others is the test of a true gentleman.

The power which the strong have over the weak, the magistrate over the citizen, the employer over the employed, the educated over the unlettered, the experienced over the confiding, even the clever over the silly —the forbearing or inoffensive use of all this power of authority, or the total absence of it when the case admits it, will show the gentleman in plain light.

The gentleman does not needlessly or unnecessarily remind an offender of a wrong he may have committed against him. He can not only forgive, he can forget; and he strives for that nobleness of self and mildness of character which impart sufficient strength to let the past be the past.

A true gentleman of honor feels humbled himself when he cannot help humbling others." [115]

PORTRAITS
★ ★ ★

Taken in early 1863 in Richmond, Virginia, this is Lee's first formal portrait as a Confederate General.

Photo by Minnis and Cowell. Provided courtesy of Special Collections, Leyburn Library, Washington and Lee University, Lexington, Virginia, 0-64-Box 27, f.8.

Lee on Traveller in Petersburg, Virginia, 1864.

Provided courtesy of Special Collections, Leyburn Library, Washington and Lee University, Lexington, Virginia, 0-64-Box 27, f12.

Taken on the back porch of his rented house at
707 East Franklin Street, Richmond, Virginia on
April 16, 1865.

Photo by Mathew Brady. Provided courtesy of Special
Collections, Leyburn library, Washington and Lee University,
Lexington, Virginia, 0-64-Box 27, f.15.

Photo by M. Miley. Provided courtesy of Robert E. Lee Collection, Special Collections, Leyburn Library, Washington and Lee University, Lexington, Virginia, 064-Box 27, f.40-C.

Protrait by Hatie E. Burdette. Provided courtesy of Special Collection, Leyburn Library, Washington and Lee University, Lexington, Virginia, 064-Box 27, f.37a.

FAITH

★ ★ ★

"Now faith is the substance of things hoped for, the evidence of things not seen. For by it the elders obtained a good report. Through faith we understand that the worlds were framed by the word of God, so that things which are seen were not made of things which do appear."

Hebrews 11:1-3, KJV

DEATH

"DEATH IN ITS SILENT, SURE MARCH IS FAST GATHERING THOSE WHOM I HAVE LONGEST LOVED, SO THAT WHEN HE SHALL KNOCK AT MY DOOR I WILL MORE WILLINGLY FOLLOW." [116]

"...we failed, but in the good providence of God apparent failure often proves a blessing." [117]

"...you must learn to be good. Be true, kind, and generous, and pray earnestly to God to enable you to 'keep his commandments, and walk in the same all the days of your life.'" [118]

"...our God mixes in the cup he gives us to drink in the World, the sweet with the bitter." [119]

"...in the end I trust all things will work together for our good." [120]

"If I could only know that all the young men in the college were good Christians, I should have nothing more to desire. I dread the thought of any student going away from college without becoming a sincere Christian." [121]

"In God alone must be our trust." [122]

"I am ought concerned with results. God's will out to be our aim, and I am quite contented that [His] designs should be accomplished and not mine." [123]

"May God bless us all and preserve us for the time when we too, must part, the one from the other, which is now close at hand, and may we all meet again at the footstool of a merciful God, to be joined by His eternal love never more to separate." [134]

"…if it is true as taught by history, that greatness rests upon virtue, it is equally true that religion is the fountain & support of virtue." [125]

Teaching

"The selection of proper persons for the office of teachers is a matter of the first importance, & as its duties require love & comprehensive preparation, it should be regarded as among the most honourable & important professions, & be committed to those whose beneficial influence & instruction shall extend to morals & religion as well as intellect. The teacher should be the example to the pupil. He should aim at the highest attainable proficiency & not at pleasing mediocrity..."[126]

"My daily prayer to the great Ruler of the world is that he may shield you from all future harm, guard you from all evil, and give you that peace which the world cannot take away." [127]

"Let us all so live that we may be united in that world where there is no more separation, and where sorrow and pain never come." [128]

"What a beautiful world God, in His loving kindness to His creatures, has given us! What a shame that men endowed with reason and knowledge of right should mar His gifts…" [129]

"We must trust all then to him…" [130]

"…while always willing to give you any advice in my power, in whatever you do you must feel that the whole responsibility rests with you…. I wish, my dear son, I could be of some advantage to you, but I can only give you my love and earnest prayers, and commit you to the keeping of that God who never forgets those who serve Him." [131]

"Above all things, learn at once to worship your Creator and to do His will as revealed in His Holy Book." [132]

"I pray that our merciful Father in Heaven may protect and direct us! In that case, I fear no odds and no numbers." [133]

"My interest in Time and its concerns is daily fading away and I try to keep my eyes and thoughts fixed on those eternal shores to which I am fast hastening." [134]

"...may the blessings of kind Heaven accompany you throughout your course on earth, & may a merciful Providence shield you from all evil, & lead you at the end to everlasting joy & peace." [135]

"May God rescue us from the folly of our acts. Save us from selfishness, and teach us to love our neighbors as ourselves." [134]

"The Chair of Mental & Moral Philosophy in Washington College...should be properly filled. The occupant should not only be a man of true piety, learning, & science; but should be so thoroughly imbued with the Heavenly principles of the blessed Gospel of Christ; as to make His Holy religion attractive to the young, to impress it upon their hearts, & to make them humble Christian." [137]

"I daily pray to the Giver of all victories..." [138]

TRUST

"How it will all end I cannot say, but will trust to a kind providence, who will, I believe, order all things for the best." [139]

"How good God is to us! Oh that I could praise Him & thank Him as I ought." [140]

"God alone can save us from our folly, selfishness & short sightedness...." [141]

"I grieve over the death of my darling little niece. How our pleasures in life go out.... May God have mercy on us & make us ready & anxious to follow her." [142]

"This is Easter Sunday. I hope you have been able to attend the services at Church. My own have been performed alone in my tent, I hope with a humble, grateful, and penitent heart, and will be acceptable to our Heavenly Father. May he continue his mercies to us both and all our children, relatives and friends, and in his own good time unite us in his worship, if not on earth, forever in heaven." [143]

"I look forward to better days, and trust that time and experience, the great teachers of men, under the guidance of an ever-merciful God, may save us from destruction, and restore us the bright hopes and prospects of the past." [144]

"Every beat of our hearts marks our progress though life and admonishes us of the steps we make towards the grave. We are thus every moment reminded to prepare for our summons." [145]

"I must ask the favour of you to thank them most heartily for their kindness in providing me a book [the Bible] in comparison with which all others in my eyes, are of minor importance and which in all my perplexities has never failed to give me light and strength." [146]

"I enjoyed the mountains as I rode along. The views were magnificent. The valleys so peaceful, the scenery so beautiful! What a glorious world Almighty God has given us! How thankless and ungrateful we are! [147]

"…our hope and refuge is in our merciful Father in heaven." [148]

"Our life in this world is of no value except to prepare us for a better. That should be our constant aim & the end of all our efforts." [149]

"Kiss your mother for me & take good care of her. You know I can do nothing for her now. Remember me in your sweet prayers & supplicate the throne of grace for mercy & forgiveness towards me. May God guard you & protect you, prays your devoted father…" [150]

"Young men must not expect to escape contact with evil, but must learn not to be contaminated by it. That virtue is worth but little that requires constant watching and removal from temptation." [151]

"We are all in the hands of our Merciful God, whom I know will order all things for our good, but we do not know what that is or what He may determine, & it behooves us to use the perception and judgement he has given us for our guidance & well being." [152]

"…upon Him is my whole faith & reliance." [153]

"God takes care of us all & calls to him those he prefers." [154]

"teach him that his only refuge is in Him, the greatness of whose mercy reacheth unto the heavens, and His truth unto the clouds." [155]

"We must…commit ourselves in adversity to the will of a merciful God as cheerfully as in prosperity." [156]

"…we must implore the forgiveness of God for our sins, & the continuance of His blessings. There is nothing but His almighty power that can sustain us." [157]

"No one can be made more sensible of their [sins] than I am. But it is so difficult to regulate your conduct. Man's nature is so selfish, so weak, every feeling & every passion urging him to folly, excess & sin [so] I am disgusted with myself & sometimes the world….Even in my progress I fail, & my only hope is in my confidence, my trust in the mercy of God which is deep and unbounded." [158]

"May God bless you my dear daughter, strew your path in this world with every happiness, & finally gather you & all of us to His mansions of bliss in heaven, is my daily & hourly prayer!" [159]

Anguish

"I cannot express the anguish I feel at the death of our sweet Annie. To know that I shall never see her again on earth, that her place in our circle, which I always hoped one day to enjoy, is forever vacant, is agonizing in the extreme. But God in this, as in all things, has mingled mercy with the blow in selecting that one best prepared to leave us. May you be able to join me in saying, "His will be done!" [160]

"The death of my dear Annie was indeed to me a bitter pang, 'but the Lord gave and the Lord has taken away, blessed be the name of the Lord.' In the quiet hours of the night, when there is nothing to lighten the full weight of my grief, I feel as if I should be overwhelmed." [161]

"Life is indeed gliding away and I have nothing good to show for mine that is past. I pray I may be spared to accomplish something for the good of mankind and the glory of God." [162]

"….some good is always mixed with the evil in this world…." [163]

"You must pray to the great God who rideth in the heavens, to give us strength & courage to do the work he has set before us, & to Him be all the praise!" [164]

"I think we should enjoy all the amenities of life that are within our reach, and which have been provided for us by our Heavenly Father...." [165]

"...people must help themselves, or Providence will not help them." [166]

"One of the miseries of war is that there is no Sabbath." [167]

"It has pleased God to take from us one exceedingly dear to us, and we must be resigned to His holy will." [168]

"Thus is link by link the strong chain broken that binds us to earth, and our passage soothed to another world. Oh, that we may be at least united in that heaven of rest, where trouble and sorrow never enter, to join in an everlasting chorus of praise to our Lord and Savior! [169]

A Brighter World

"THE TIES TO EARTH ARE TAKEN, ONE BY ONE, BY OUR MERCIFUL GOD TO TURN OUR HEARTS TO HIM AND TO SHOW US THAT THE OBJECT OF THIS LIFE IS TO PREPARE FOR A BETTER AND BRIGHTER WORLD. MAY WE ALL BE THERE UNITED TO PRAISE AND WORSHIP HIM FOREVER AND EVER!" [170]

The Word

"There are many things in the [Bible] which I may never be able to explain, but I accept it as the infallible Word of God, and receive its teachings as inspired by the Holy Ghost." [171]

"I can only say that I am nothing but a poor sinner, trusting in Christ alone for salvation…." [172]

"No day should be lived unless it was begun with a prayer of thankfulness and an intercession for guidance." [173]

"One of the best ways that I know to induce the students to attend chapel is to be sure we attend ourselves." [174]

"…we must not repine, but be resigned, knowing that [God] will not afflict us but for our own good." [175]

"We are all prone I think to undervalue the gifts of a merciful God, & to make our own unhappiness. I am conscious of my faults in this respect & make many resolutions & attempts to do better, but fail. I will continue my efforts & am resolved to improve." [176]

"My trust is in the mercy & wisdom of a kind Providence who ordereth all things for our good, & who can guard & protect us whether united or separate." [177]

"My chief concern is to try to be a humble, sincere Christian myself." [178]

"God helps those who help themselves in his own good time." [179]

"The best way for most of us is to fast from our sins and to eat what is good for us." [180]

Leave Without Regret

"...Find time to read and improve your mind. Read history, works of truth...Get correct views of life, and learn to see the world in its true light, it will enable you to live pleasantly, to do good, and, when summoned away, to leave without regret." [181]

WHO IS THIS MAN
ROBERT E. LEE?

"…the tribunal of mankind
can judge this man,
who was born not for a period,
but for all time;
not for a country, but for the world;
not for a people,
but for the human race." [183]

—John Hampden Chamberlayne
(Captain C.S.A), January 19, 1876

"What he seemed he was…" [184]

Douglas Southall Freeman, Lee biographer

"He had all the great virtues.
His dignity of demeanor, his courtesy,
his savoir faire, were remarkable.
To us he was an Olympian,
seen in a haze of great deeds.
We knew him as a just, firm,
polite administrator,
whose lightest word was law.
The respect for him was profound.
He could do no wrong.
We likened him to Agamemon,
and we were his Achaioi,
battling on the windy plains of Troy.
Spiritually, he thoroughly dominated us." [185]

Dr. Samuel Z. Ammen, Baltimore, Maryland

*Ammen joined four other classmates inspired
by the character of Lee to form the Kappa
Alpha Order at Washington College while
Lee was president.*

*The Kappa Alpha Order honors Lee today
as their "spiritual founder."*

CHARACTER

★ ★ ★

It was Lee's biographer Douglas Southall Freeman who posed and briefly answered in his pamphlet, The Lengthening Shadow of Lee: " How is it," he asked, "that his shadow lengthens daily? The answer is to the honor of mankind. A generation sometimes mistakes the theatrical for the dramatic, the specious for the serious, the pretender for the defender. The 'hero of the hour' may not have deserved his place even for that hour; he who is a hero when his century is done has qualities that are timeless." [186]

"I have met many of the great men of my time, but Lee alone impressed me with the feeling that I was in the presence of a man who was cast in grander mould, and made of different and of finer metal than all other men." [187]

Englishman Field Marshall Viscount Wolseley

"Without any exception the very greatest of all the great captains that the English-speaking peoples have brought forth." [188]

President Theodore Roosevelt

"One of the noblest Americans who ever lived, and one of the greatest captains known to the annals of war." [189]

Winston Churchill

"The most stainless of living commanders, and, excepting in fortune, the greatest..." [190]

Philip Stanhope Worsley, British poet and scholar

"Lee was a great person, not so much because of what he did (although his accomplishments were extraordinary); he was great because of the way he lived, because of what he was." [191]

Emory M. Thomas

"To us he was what a true and loving father is to his children, guide, counselor, benefactor, and devoted friend... It would be difficult to conceive of a nobler presence or a more attractive personality than his! A form of 'noblest mold' crowned by a countenance perfect in its calm benignity, and manly beauty. Large lustrous dark brown eyes, kindly eyes— honest, earnest eyes—which you saw at once were the windows of a great soul... A bearing, simple, graceful, and natural, in which there was modesty without diffidence, and supreme dignity without self-assertion." [192]

Wm. A. Anderson, Rector of Washington and Lee University

"He did not use tobacco in any form, nor partake of intoxicating liquors… He never used slang nor told a joke which his wife and daughters might not have listened to with perfect propriety." [193]

Edward Clifford Gordon, St. Louis, Missouri

"He had unquestionably great delicacy and tenderness of feeling, constantly manifested in his regard for animals, his love for children, his consideration for the distressed." [194]

Edward Clifford Gordon, St. Louis, Missouri

"He remembered every child in Lexington whose name he had heard and whose face he had seen." [195]

Edward Clifford Gordon, St. Louis, Missouri

"I have known men who knew more Latin, Greek, mathematics and philosophy than he did; but I never knew any one who knew men as well as he did. There was something uncanny about his ability to read other men's thoughts." [196]

Edward Clifford Gordon, St. Louis, Missouri

"He himself 'toed the mark,' and he insisted that everybody else should do the same." [197]

Edward Clifford Gordon, St. Louis, Missouri

"In his home he was the most courteous of hosts." [198]

Edward Clifford Gordon, St. Louis, Missouri

"I have seen him in garments which many men of smaller income and far less reputation would have been unwilling to wear." [199]

Edward Clifford Gordon, St. Louis, Missouri

"I pass on to record his high regard for what was just, right and honorable…high and noble characteristics were constantly manifested in the conduct of his private business. They caused him to refuse over and over again the use of his name in business enterprises after the war when he was desirous of work which would enable him to provide for his family. Large sums of money were offered to him only for the use of his name. He was to have no work, no trouble, no responsibility. It was the absence of these things which made him decline these flattering offers." [200]

Edward Clifford Gordon, St. Louis, Missouri

"…it seemed to me, he had never done anything of which he was ashamed and which it was necessary for him to conceal…" [201]

Edward Clifford Gordon, St. Louis, Missouri

"The supreme test of a man's greatness is his ability to control other men; to draw them to himself, to secure their constant loyalty, to have them execute his will. General Lee stood this test." [202]

Edward Clifford Gordon, St. Louis, Missouri

"The world already knows how prone he was at all times to take upon his own shoulders the responsibility for failure or mishap, and thus shield those from censure who had really failed..." [203]

Walter H. Taylor,
C.S.A. lieutenant colonel & aide to Lee

"He was then at the zenith of his physical beauty. Admirably proportioned, of graceful and dignified carriage, with strikingly handsome features, bright and penetrating eyes, his iron-gray hair closely cut, his face cleanly shaved except a mustache, he appeared every inch a soldier and a man born to command." [204]

Walter H. Taylor, describing Lee when they first met
C.S.A. lieutenant colonel & aide to Lee

"Such was Robert E. Lee: a man great and good among the greatest and best of the sons of men…His most intimate friends, his bitterest enemies, sought in vain to find any seriously weak spot in his character… He devoted his life, his matchless abilities, to impersonal ends: not to be served but to serve." [205]

Edward Clifford Gordon, St. Louis, Missouri

"Of all men I have ever known, I think General R. E. Lee by far the greatest as a soldier, a citizen, and executive officer and Christian gentleman. In my humble opinion he stands without a superior...His influence over the whole body of students was remarkable...In discipline he was firm and exacting, but kind and just. Socially, he was very genial, cordial and very entertaining in conversation." [206]

Mr. C.W. Hedger, Sweet Springs, Missouri

"There was no time that he ever failed to recognize me, and had always a kindly word of cheer to say at the right moment...General Lee as college president was great because of his sympathetic touch..." [207]

Rev. James R. Winchester, Little Rock, Arkansas

"To the youth he was indeed a father, gently admonishing, if wayward, encouraging, if backward, and praising, if successful, — always mindful of our moral and physical welfare. To the mature he was both friend and counselor, exercising the same watchful care—encouraging, complimenting, and admonishing, if necessary. To all he was the same, a peerless model, influencing by wise precept and noble example." [208]

Mr. Hubbard G. Carlton, Richmond, Virginia

"He was almost a second father to me…To me he was the grandest of men. His unobtrusive demeanor; his dignity and gentleness; his firmness in and devotion to principle, elevated, graced and gave dignity to official and personal associations." [209]

Mr. Willa Viley, Wiley, Georgia

"The students and entire population of Lexington had not only the highest respect but the deepest love for General Lee. One cause for this was the very real interest he took in everyone." [210]

Mr. John R. Ponder, Los Angeles, California

"My reverence for the great soldier deepened into a personal attachment for the noble gentleman, the kind and gracious friend, so human and sympathetic with all his greatness. His very presence seemed to make purer the atmosphere around him, and there was in him a blended dignity and sweetness that made a man feel better for the seeing. His influence with the wildest and most careless was wonderful, and yet no harsh word fell from his lips." [211]

Judge D. Gardiner Tyler, Holdcroft, Virginia

"His quiet, kindly manner when talking to a student, was always profoundly impressive…His spirit overshadowed everything about the college and the community." [212]

Dr. Chalmers Dedrick, Knoxville, Tennessee

"Those who had the privilege of his personal acquaintance at once recognize a character in which were blended the noblest qualities of mind and heart." [213]

Edward V. Valentine, Richmond, Virginia —
sculptor of the Lee "Recumbent Statue"

"Sir, he is the noblest man that ever lived. He not only had a kind word for an old soldier who fought against him, but he gave me some money to help me on my way." [214]

A union soldier after the war

"As a soldier, General Lee left his mark on military strategy. As a man, he stood as the symbol of valor and of duty. As an educator, he appealed to reason and learning to achieve understanding and to build a stronger nation. The course he chose after the war became a symbol to all those who had marched with him in the bitter years towards Appomattox...General Lee's character has been an example to succeeding generations..." [215]

President Gerald R. Ford restoring Lee's rights of citizenship
August 5, 1975

"...a leader of men in war and peace, a champion of principles, a humanitarian, a man who devoted his entire life to the benefit of others without regard to himself. Time after time, he was offered opportunities to gain fame and wealth, but neither factor influenced his decision to take a course of action he conscientiously believed to be right." [216]

President Woodrow Wilson

"We use the word 'great' indiscriminately … but we reserve the word 'noble' carefully for those whose greatness is not spent in their own interest … that was the characteristic of General Lee's life." [217]

President Woodrow Wilson

"My dear boys…as the characters of great men are valuable guides to growing boys who are shaping their own, I will take this occasion to tell you something about the famous Commander of the Army of Northern Virginia, General Lee…I have always observed that you can tell the character of a man by his eyes, and I would be willing to stake my farm and all I am worth upon the statement that there never was a person with such eyes as General Lee's who was not an honest man…" [218]

Corporal Shabrach, Army of Northern Virginia
December 10, 1863- letter to his sons

"His office was always open to students or professors, all of whose interest received his ready consideration…under the inspiration of his central influence, the utmost harmony and the utmost energy pervaded all the departments of the College. The highest powers of both professors and students were called forth, under the fullest responsibility." [219]

Dr. J.W. Jones

"In the discipline of the College his moral influence was supreme…In his construction of college rules, and his dealings with actions generally, he was most liberal; but in his estimate of motives, and in the requirement of principle and honor, he was exacting to the last degree. Youthful indiscretion found in him the most lenient of judges; but falsehood or meanness had no toleration with him…he was always the last to condemn, and the most just to hear the truth, even in behalf of the worst offender…His reproof was stern, yet kind, and often even melting in his tenderness; and his appeals, always addressed to the noblest motives, were irresistible. The hardiest offenders were alike awed by his presence, and moved, often to tears, by his words…His discipline was moral rather than punitive…the need for such punishments became ever less and less. The influence of this policy, aided especially by the mighty influence of his personal character, was all-powerful. The elevation of tone, and the improvement in conduct, were steady and rapid…The whole College, in a word, felt his influence as an ever-present motive, and his character was quietly yet irresistibly impressed upon it…" [220]

Dr. J.W. Jones

"He knew all of the children in Lexington, and along the roads…of his daily rides, and it was pleasing to witness their delight when they met him." [221]

Dr. J.W. Jones

"I knew there was no use to urge him to do anything against his ideas of what was right." [222]

U.S. Grant

"General Lee had but one manner in his intercourse with men. It was the same to the peasant as to the prince…" [223]

John B. Collyar, Nashville, Tennessee

"Character is invincible—that, it seems to me, is the life of Robert E. Lee in three words." [224]

Douglas Southall Freeman, Lee biographer

"Robert E. Lee was one of the small company of great men in whom there is no inconsistency to be explained, no enigma to be solved. What he seemed he was—a wholly human gentleman, the essential elements of whose positive character were two and two only, simplicity and spirituality." [225]

Douglas Southall Freeman, Lee biographer

"...he was the only man I ever met who measured up to my concept of Washington. The grandeur of his appearance is beyond my power of portraiture. He is ineffable." [226]

James C. Nisbet, Georgia

"Like Niagara, the more you gazed the more his grandeur grew upon you, the more his majesty expanded and filled your spirit with a full satisfaction that left a perfect delight without the slightest feeling of oppression. Grandly majestic and dignified in all his deportment..." [227]

General John B. Gordon

"...he had a power to bring out, and did bring out, the very best that was in every student." [228]

A Washington College student while Lee was president

"To approach him was to feel in the presence of a man of superior intellect, possessing the capacity to accomplish great ends, and the gift of controlling and leading men." [229]

Major John S. Ford, Texas Rangers

"In youth & early manhood I loved and admired him more than any man in the world...No other youth or man so united the qualities that win warm friendship and command high respect. For he was full of sympathy and kindness, genial and fond of gay conversation, and even of fun, while his correctness of demeanor and attention to duties...gave him superiority that every one acknowledged in his heart." [230]

Joseph E. Johnston, Lee's West Point roommate, friend and Confederate general

FAITH

★ ★ ★

"Lee the soldier was great but Lee the man and Christian was greater by far." [231]

Douglas Southall Freeman, Lee Biographer

"Here he now sleeps in the land he loved so well…This good citizen, this gallant soldier, this great general, this true patriot, had yet a higher praise than this or these, he was a true Christian…Our loss is not his, for he now enjoys the rewards of a life well spent…his deeds will be remembered; and when the monument we build shall have crumbled into dust, his virtues will still live, a high model for the imitation of generations yet unborn." [232]

Jefferson Davis-speech at the November 3, 1870 Lee Memorial Meeting, Richmond VA

"To the faculty he was an elder brother, beloved and revered, and full of all tender sympathy. To the students, he was a father, in carefulness, in encouragement, in reproof. Their welfare and their conduct and character as gentlemen, were his chief concern...He thought it to be the office of a college not merely to educate the intellect, but to make Christian men. The moral and religious character of the students was more precious in his eyes even than their intellectual progress..." [233]

Dr. J.W. Jones

"...he was absolutely stainless in his private life. I did not know then, as I do now, that he had been a model youth and young man; but I had before me the most manly man and entire gentleman I ever met...I met him at times later, and he was always the same Christian gentleman." [234]

Alexander H. Stevens, vice-president of the Confederacy

"…a simple man whose character grew in proportion to his commitment to the life-task he felt God had assigned him…" [235]

Clifford Dowdey

"Lee's genius was essentially military; but his greatness was essentially religious." [236]

Marshall W. Fishwick

"If I have ever come in contact with a sincere devout Christian—one who seeing himself as a sinner, trusted alone in the merits of Christ, who humbly tried to walk the path of duty, 'Looking unto Jesus as the author and finisher of his faith, and whose piety constantly exhibited itself in his daily life—that man was General Robert E. Lee." [237]

Reverend J. William Jones, Baptist minister and close friend

"I speak from intimate personal acquaintance when I write on the Christian character of Robert E. Lee, the greatest soldier of history, and the model man of the centuries…He was emphatically a man of prayer… He was a devout and constant Bible reader, and found time to read the old book even amid his most pressing duties." [238]

Rev. J. William Jones

"During and after the war General Lee manifested in the highest degree the Christian spirit of forgiveness. He hated all wrong and wrongdoing …" [239]

Edward Clifford Gordon, St. Louis, Missouri

" What he was, I ardently wish all men could be." [240]

W.W. Estill

A Washington College student while Lee was president

"… in all the elements of true greatness General Lee was far in advance of any man I had ever known… If extensive knowledge, if far-seeing wisdom, if a wonderous self-control, if ability to manage great enterprises and to master minute details, if the spirit of meekness and of self-sacrifice, if simplicity in thought and speech, if courtesy and an exquisite sense of honor, if ability to estimate other men and to mold them to his will, are elements of greatness, then General Lee was, and is, my beau-ideal of the highest type of Christian gentleman." [241]

Edward Clifford Gordon, St. Louis, Missouri

"He loved and honored his own church and supported it heartily with his money and his example...The religious phase of his character may be summed up in three short sentences. He trusted and loved God. He loved his fellow men. He believed in Jesus Christ as his Saviour and Lord, and manifested the Christian spirit towards enemies as well as friends." [242]

Edward Clifford Gordon, St. Louis, Missouri

"He is an illustrious example of those whose clear moral judgments no glory can obscure; whose integrity no temptation can corrupt. He is an epistle, written of God and designed by God to teach the people of this country that earthly success is not the criterion of merit, nor the measure of true greatness." [243]

Edward Clifford Gordon, St. Louis, Missouri

WHO IS THIS MAN
ROBERT E. LEE?

By Curt Steger
Mt. Sterling, Kentucky, 2006

Who is this man Robert E. Lee
Father of seven children
And last father of The South?

Who is this man Robert E. Lee
Whose "lengthening shadow" falls on humanity
More than a century after his death?

Who is this man Robert E. Lee
Whose words bring comfort and wisdom
And cause reflection to those that read them?

Who is this man Robert E. Lee
Who knew who he was
When his world around him
Did not know what it was?

Who is this man Robert E. Lee
Who still inspires men of all ages
To become different and better men?

Who is this man Robert E. Lee?
He is every man with principles
based on character and faith
He is you and he is me
If we will but let him be.

ENDNOTES

1. Joseph H. Crute, Jr. The Derwent Letter, (Powhatan, Virginia: Derwent Books, 1985) 23
2. Clifford Dowdey and Louis H. Manarian, The Wartime Papers of Robert E. Lee (Boston: Da Capo Press, 1961) 395-396.
3. Margaret Sanborn, Robert E. Lee: A Portrait (Moose, Wyoming: Homestead Publishing, 1966, 1996) 174.
4. Robert E. Lee, Jr., Recollections and Letters of General Robert E. Lee (New York, Doubleday, 1904) 303.
5. J. William Jones, Life and Letters of Gen. Robert Edward Lee: Soldier And Man (Harrisburg, Virginia: Sprinkle Publications,1906) 460.
6. Ibid. 110.
7. Lee, Recollections and Letters of General R. E. Lee 67.
8. Mary P Coulling, The Lee Girls (Winston-Salem: John F. Publisher, 1987) 75.
9. Fitzhugh Lee, General Lee: A Biography of Robert E. Lee (Boston: Da Capo Press, 1894) 66.
10. Devereaux D. Cannon, Jr. The Wit and Wisdom of Robert E. Lee (Gretna, Louisiana: Pelican Publishing Co., 1997) 22.
11. Douglas Southall Freeman, R.E. Lee: A Biography, 4 vols. (New York: Charles Scribner's Sons, 1934) 4:314.
12. The Lee Papers, Photostat #247, Leyburn Library, Washington & Lee University, Lexington, VA.
13. Lee, Recollections and Letters of General R.E. Lee 151.
14. Emory M. Thomas, Robert E. Lee: A Biography (New York: W.W. Norton & Company 1995) 150.
15. Freeman, R.E.Lee 4:296.
16. Thomas, R.E.Lee: A Biography 116.
17. Lee, Recollections and Letters of General R. E. Lee 15.
18. Cannon, Wit and Wisdom of R E.Lee 19.
19. H.W. Crocker III, Robert E. Lee On Leadership (Rocklin: California: Forum-Prima Publishing 1999) 188.
20. Clifford Dowdey, Lee (Gettysburg: Stan Clark Military Books 1965) 144.
21. Lee, Recollections and Letters of General R. E. Lee 358
22. The Lee Papers, Photostat #192, Leyburn Library, Washington and lee University, Lexington, Virginia
23. Dowdey, Lee 514
24. Ibid.
25. Jones, Life and Letters of General R. E. Lee 96
26. Cannon, Wit and Wisdom of R.E. Lee 40.
27. Lee, Biography of Robert E. Lee 65
28. Ibid.
29. Ibid.
30. Ibid.
31. Lee, Recollections and Letters of General R. E. Lee 333.
32. Cannon, Wit and Wisdom of R.E. Lee 32.
33. Ibid. 44.
34. Freeman, R.E. Lee 4:433.
35. Lee, Recollections and Letters of General R.E. Lee 253.
36. Ibid.
37. Thomas, R.E. Lee: A Biography 169.
38. Cannon, Wit and Wisdom of R.E. Lee 24.
39. Lee, Recollections and Letters of General R. E. Lee 257.
40. Lee, Biography of Robert E. Lee 130-131.
41. Ibid.
42. Jones, Life and Letters of General R.E. Lee 354.
43. The Lee Papers, Photostat #244, Leyburn Library, Washington and Lee University, Lexington, VA.
44. Jones, Life and Letters of General R.E. Lee 160.
45. Michael Fellman, The Making of Robert E. Lee (New York: Random House, 2000) 41.
46. Ibid. 47-48
47. Freeman, R.E. Lee 4:182.
48. Dowdey et al, Wartime Papers of R.E. Lee 652.
49. Sanborn, R.E. Lee: A Portrait 420
50. Dowdey et al, Wartime Papers of R.E. Lee 105.
51. Rod Cragg, A Commitment To Valor: A Character Portrait of Robert E Lee (Nashville, TN: Rutledge Hill Press, 2001) 242.
52. Lee, Recollections and Letters of General R.E. Lee 319.
53. Freeman, R.E. Lee 3:155.
54. Dowday, Lee 698.
55. Fellman, The Making of R.E. Lee 171.
56. Ibid.
57. Crute, The Derwent Letters 28.
58. Ibid. 29.
59. Dowdey et al, Wartime Papers of R.E. Lee 678.
60. Lee. Biography of Robert E. Lee 63.
61. Thomas, R.E. Lee: A Biography 152
62. Fellman, The Making of R.E. Lee 42.
63. Sanborn, R.E. Lee: A Portrait 183.
64. The Lee Papers, #187, Leyburn Library, Washington and Lee University, Lexington, Virginia.

65. Sanborn, R.E. Lee: A Portrait 215.
66. Ibid. 425
67. Robert R. Brown, And One Was A Soldier (Shippenburg, PA: White Maine Publishing 1998) 56
68. Sanborn, R.E. Lee: A Portrait 73.
69. A.L. Long, Memoirs of Robert E. Lee (New York: J. M. Stoddart & Company 1886)454.
70. Freeman, R.E. Lee 4:278
71. Sanborn, R.E. Lee: A Portrait 346.
72. Dowdey et al, Wartime Papers of R.E. Lee 240.
73. Jones, Life and Letters of General R.E. Lee 279.
74. Brown, And One Was A Soldier 57
75. Dowdey et al, Wartime Papers of R.e. lee 597-598.
76. Ibid.
77. Ibid.
78. Lee, Recollections and Letters of General R. E. Lee 432-433.
79. Sanborn, R.E. Lee: A Portrait 167.
80. Ibid.
81. Ibid. 73.
82. Ibid. 77.
83. Freeman, R.E. Lee 3:254.
84. Jones, Life and Letters of General R.E. Lee 117.
85. Freeman, R.E. Lee 4:281.
86. Ibid.
87. The Lee Papers, #233, Leyburn Library, Washington and Lee University, Lexington, Virginia.
88. Cragg, A Commitment To Valor 24.
89. J.Steven Wilkins, Call of Duty: The Sterling Nobility of Robert E. Lee (Nashville, Tennessee: Cumberland House, 1997) 323.
90. Freeman, R.E. Lee 4:280.
91. Cragg, A Commitment To Valor 46.
92. Ibid. 43.
93. Ibid. 26.
94. Ibid. 41.
95. Ibid. 25.
96. Franklin L. Riley, Robert E. Lee After Appomattox (New York, Macmillan, 1922-) 18.
97. Ibid. 25.
98. Sanborn, R.E. Lee: A Portrait 396
99. Thomas L. Connelly, The Marble Man: Robert E. Lee and His Image in American Society (Baton Rouge: Louisiana State University Press, 1977) 189.
100. Cragg, A Commitment To Valor 18
101. Thomas L. Connelly, The Marble Man: Robert E. Lee and His Image in American Society (Baton Rouge: Louisiana State University Press, 1977) 189.
102. Ibid. 174.
103. Freeman, R.E. Lee 3:330-331.
104. Jones, Life and Letters of General R.E. Lee 113.
105. Ibid.
106. Connelly, The Marble Man 179.
107. Ibid.
108. Ibid.
109. Riley, R.E. Lee After Appomattox 92.
110. Dowdey et al, Wartime Papers of R.E. Lee 53.
111. Long, memoirs of Robert E. Lee
112. Riley, R.E. Lee After Appomattox 154.
113. Richard B. McCaslin, Lee in the Shadow of Washington (Baton Rouge: Louisiana State University Press 2001) 217.
114. Lee, recollections and Letters of General R.E. Lee 247
115. Crocker, R.E. Lee On Leadership 177.
116. Freeman, R.E. Lee 4:272
117. Ibid. 401-402
118. Jones, Life and Letters of General R.E. Lee 40.
119. Freeman, R.E. Lee 4:257
120. Ibid. 315
121. Ibid. 426
122. Wilkins, Call of Duty 93
123. Ibid.
124. Freeman, R.E. Lee 4:434
125. The Lee Papers, #187:original, Leyburn Library, Washington and Lee University, Lexington, Virginia
126. Ibid.
127. Lee, Recollections and letters of General R.E. Lee 268.
128. Ibid. 260
129. Ibid 96
130. Ibid. 32.

131. Ibid. 236-237.
132. Freeman, R.E. Lee 4:270.
133. Lee, Recollections and Letters of General R.E. Lee 95
134. Freeman, R.E. Lee 4:345
135. Ibid. 410
136. Jones, Life and Letters of General R.E. Lee 122.
137. The Lee Papers, #147, Leyburn Library, Washington and Lee University, Lexington, Virginia.
138. Lee, Recollections and Letters of General R.E. Lee 63.
139. Lee, Biography of Robert E. Lee 44.
140. Dowdey et al, Wartime Papers of R.E. Lee 680.
141. Alan T. Nolan, Lee Considered; General Robert E. Lee and Civil War History (Chapel Hill:The University of North Carolina Press, 1991) 33.
142. Dowdey et al, Wartime Papers of R.E. Lee 888.
143. Lee, Biography of Robert E. Lee 68.
144. Crute, The Derwent Letters 22.
145. J. Williams Jones, Christ In The Camp (Harrisonburg, Virginia: Sprinkle Publications) 68
146. Lee, Recollections and Letters of General R.E. Lee 217.
147. Jones, Life and Letters of General R.E. Lee 145.
148. Lee, Biography of Robert E. Lee 314.
149. Dowdey et al, Wartime Papers of R.E. Lee 705.
150. Ibid. 493.
151. Cannon, Wit and Wiscom of R.E. Lee 24.
152. Dowdey et al, Wartime Papers of R.E. Lee 765.
153. Ibid.
154. Ibid. 511
155. Ibid. 512.
156. Sanborn, R.E. Lee: A Portrait 400.
157. Dowdey et al, Wartime Papers of R.E. Lee 551.
158. Fellman, The Making of R.E. Lee 50
159. Ibid. 561-562.
160. Lee, Recollections and Letters of General R.E. Lee 98.
161. Lee, Recollections and Letters of General R.E. Lee 189.
162. Dowdey et al, Wartime Papers of R.E. Lee 623-624.
163. Lee, Recollections and Letters of General R.E. Lee 197.
164. Lee, Biography of Robert E. Lee 234
165. Jones, Life and Letters of General R.E. lee 199.
166. Dowdey et al, Wartime papers of R.E. Lee 350-351.
167. Lee, Recollections and Letters of General R.E. Lee 56
168. Freeman, R.E. Lee 3:217
169. Ibid.
170. Jones, Life and Letters of General R.E. Lee 297.
171. Cragg, A Commitment To Valor 114.
172. Ibid. 112.
173. Ibid.
174. Ibid. 36.
175. Connelly, The Marble Man 190-191.
176. Avery Craven, "To Markie" – The Letters of Robert E. Lee to Martha Custis Williams (Cambridge: Harvard University Press, 1933) 45-46
177. Ibid. 53.
178. Marshall Fishwick, Robert E. Lee: Churchman (Living History Series #2) 18-19.
179. Connelly, The Marble Man 181.
180. Riley, R.E. Lee After Appomattox 100.
181. Lee, Recollections and Letters of General R. E. Lee 247-248.
182. Jones, Dr. J.W., Life and letters of General Robert E. Lee (Sprinkle Publications 1986) 396.
183. Walter H. Taylor, Four Years with General Lee (Bloomington & Indianapolis: Indiana University Press, 1996) 99.
184. Thomas, R. E. Lee: A Biography 13
185. Riley, R. E. Lee After Appomattox 142-143.
186. Douglas Southhall Freeman, The Lengthening Shadow of Robert E. Lee (Richmond, Virginia: Address before Virginia General Assembly – 1937) 7-p. E467.1.L4F827.
187. Crocker, R. E. Lee On Leadership 4.
188. Ibid.
189. Ibid.
190. Sanborn, R.E.Lee: A Portrait 436
191. Thomas, R. E. Lee: A Biography 14.
192. Riley, R. E. Lee After Appomattox 197-198
193. Ibid. 78.
194. Ibid.
195. Ibid. 82.

196. Ibid. 83.
197. Ibid. 88.
198. Ibid. 90.
199. Ibid. 95.
200. Ibid. 94-95.
201. Ibid. 96.
202. Ibid. 97.
203. Taylor, Four Years With Lee 147.
204. Ibid. 3.
205. Riley, R. E. Lee After Appomattox 102-103.
206. Ibid. 111.
207. Ibid. 113.
208. Ibid. 116.
209. Ibid. 120-121.
210. Ibid. 123.
211. Ibid. 128.
212. Ibid. 135 & 137.
213. Ibid. 154-155.
214. Jones, Life & Letters of R.E.Lee 402.
215. President Gerald R. Ford Speech- August 5, 1975. Source: www.presidency.ucsb.edu
216. Connelly, The Marble Man 162.
217. President Woodrow Wilson -Source: www.Billofrightsinstitute.org
218. John Eston Cooke, The Wearing of The Gray (Bloomington: Indiana University Press, 1959) 365-372.
219. Jones, Life & Letters of R.E.Lee 422 & 424.
220. Ibid. 419-421.
221. Ibid. 464-465.
222. U.S Grant, Personal Memoirs of U.S. Grant (New York: Charles L. Webster & Company 1886) Vol. II. 497.
223. Riley, R. E. Lee After Appomattox 65.
224. Connelly, The Marble Man 153.
225. Thomas, R. E. Lee: A Biography 13.
226. Brown, And One Was A Soldier 99.
227. Ibid. 100.
228. Ibid. 101-102.
229. Sanborn, Robert E. Lee: A Portrait 204.
230. Peter S. Carmichael, Audacity Personified (Baton Rouge: Louisiana State University Press, 2004) 155 and John M. Taylor, Duty Faithfully Performed (Dulles, Virginia:Brassey's, 1999) 17.
231. David E. Johnson, Douglas Southall Freeman (Gretna, Louisiana: Pelican Publishing Company, 2002) 103.
232. Jefferson Davis- November 3, 1870-speech at the Lee Memorial Meeting-Richmond, Virginia Source: Unknown
233. Jones, Life & Letters of R.E. Lee 419.
234. Ibid. 135-136.
235. Brown, And One Was A Soldier 99.
236. Ibid.
237. Ibid. 100.
238. Riley, R. E. Lee After Appomattox 183 & 188.
239. Ibid. 101.
240. Ibid. 53.
241. Ibid. 77.
242. Ibid. 99-100.
243. Ibid. 103.